From Milk to Meat

A Primer for Christian Living

From Milk to Meat

A Primer for Christian Living

Bishop Arthur M. Brazier

 Unless otherwise identified, Scripture quotations are from the King James Version of the Bible.

Take note that the name satan and related names are not capitalized. We choose not to acknowledge him, even to the point of violating grammatical rules.

Treasure House

An Imprint of

Destiny Image® Publishers, Inc.
P.O. Box 310
Shippensburg, PA 17257-0310

"For where your treasure is
there will your heart be also." Matthew 6:21

ISBN 1-56043-278-0

For Worldwide Distribution
Printed in the U.S.A.

Treasure House books are available through these fine distributors outside the United States:

Christian Growth, Inc.
Jalan Kilang-Timor, Singapore 0315

Omega Distributors
Ponsonby, Auckland, New Zealand

Rhema Ministries Trading
Randburg, Rep. of South Africa

Salvation Book Centre
Petaling, Jaya, Malaysia

Successful Christian Living
Capetown, Rep. of South Africa

Vine Christian Centre
Mid Glamorgan, Wales, United Kingdom

WA Buchanan Company
Geebung, Queensland, Australia

Word Alive
Niverville, Manitoba, Canada

This book and all other Destiny Image
and Treasure House books
are available at Christian bookstores everywhere.

Call for a bookstore nearest you.
1-800-722-6774

Or reach us on the Internet: **http://www.reapernet.com**

For when for the time ye ought to be teachers, ye have need that one teach you again which be the first principles of the oracles of God; and are become such as have need of milk, and not of strong meat. For every one that useth milk is unskilful in the word of righteousness: for he is a babe. But strong meat belongeth to them that are of full age, even those who by reason of use have their senses exercised to discern both good and evil (Hebrews 5:12-14).

Dedication

To my father and mother, Robert F. Brazier and Geneva Brazier, who placed my feet on the path of righteousness.

Special thanks to Dr. Sammie Dortch, without whom this book would have never been written.

Contents

Preface

From Milk to Meat is a collection of excerpts from Bible classes I have taught over a 30-year period. At the insistence of the Holy Spirit, my own thinking has grown and changed during this time. This book is the result of that evolutionary process.

The individuals who deserve credit for my finally writing this book make up a list that is too long to name. The prompting to put this orally-presented material into book form came from many directions: new members in my congregation, the Apostolic Church of God, who wanted reading material covering the topics taught in the Bible classes for new members; new pastors in other congregations; seminary students in the care of our ministry; and visitors who have been interested in the approach the church takes to ministering to the needs of its members and to the unchurched through its outreach ministries.

In this work I have provided a broad introduction to a denomination that has gained a wide appeal over the last ten years. Although this work is primarily for new believers, it answers questions that have come up regularly in the Church at large, whether I was delivering a sermon in a Pentecostal church in France or in Indiana.

Some of the topics covered include the following: By Their Fruit; Not of Ourselves: The New Birth; The Sinful Nature; Except the Lord Builds the House; The Need for the Holy Spirit; Eternal Life; Security in Christ; Free Will; and Election and Security.

Introduction

Many new believers—or saints, as members of the Christian community are called by apostle Paul—have questions about what happened to them when they received Christ and heard and responded to the call to come forth to be baptized. They vaguely remember standing and moving down the aisle, seemingly without their feet touching the floor. Near the end of the aisle they were gathered into the waiting hands and arms of brothers and sisters in Christ who walked with them to the baptismal pool. New believers also wonder about what will happen after the baptism and tarry room experiences. Being filled without warning with the presence of the Holy Spirit is a never to be forgotten experience. It can be at the same time exciting and frightening. If one speaks in tongues, the mystery surrounding how and why may leave the believer feeling exhilarated and exhausted, yet also filled with questions. Upon return to the everyday world, the reality of the ever-present flesh breaks through the veil of mystery and reveals other unanswered questions such as:

How will I continue to hold onto these wonderful feelings?

Why is water baptism in Jesus' name so central to the faith?

Where are the specific instructions that will help me know what is expected of me now that I have chosen the Christian way?

How will I consistently live the life of a Christian?

Where does one who has been given "free will" draw the line?

Now that I have been saved can I be lost again?

My work for the Lord is great. However, since I am saved by grace does my good work count?

What security is there in being a saint?

From Milk to Meat introduces many of the basic doctrinal beliefs and practices that are taught, preached, and followed in a number of Pentecostal churches, particularly those that are Apostolic. It addresses some of the confusion and uncertainty felt by new saints, especially those who have previously worshiped in a different denomination. With this work I am also responding to the needs of the increasing number of "academically educated" (believers with a variety of degrees) who are seeking a "non-intellectual" form of worship, which includes the experience of speaking in tongues and other signs of spontaneous worship.

Traditionally, Pentecostal churches were looked upon as attracting worshipers who were "downtrodden" or "disinherited." However, today it is not unusual to find saints from every walk of life sitting shoulder-to-shoulder in the Pentecostal sanctuary. Furthermore, as I travel and have increased opportunity to talk and listen to the growing number of Pentecostals, I am becoming more acutely aware of the appeal of Pentecostal worship experiences. These experiences provide a balm for those of us who are seeking healing for our "sin sick" souls. This healing balm is found only in the presence of the indwelling Spirit.

The growth of Pentecostalism and the adoption of some of its practices into mainline churches, such as Baptist, Roman Catholic, and Lutheran, bear witness to the need for relief from that which we cannot ourselves escape—the emptiness that comes from separation from God. The common ground we seek is found in the communication that comes through the Holy Spirit and makes its presence known across the lines of race, gender, age, and denomination. The key to understanding the language spoken by the Holy Spirit is found in Scripture. Scripture provides us with instruction that lasts beyond the shifting winds of time. We are instructed in a way that is old, yet new.

Although there are doctrinal differences within Pentecostalism, water baptism and belief in being filled with the Holy Spirit (usually associated with speaking in tongues) are two events that are generally a basic part of this movement. Some who have experienced being filled with the Holy Spirit report that for them it resulted in deeper understanding of the love of God; desire to read and study the Bible; belief in Scripture; power to testify; and power to pray with the sick. In essence, the experience comes when the nonbeliever recognizes his or her separation from God, receives Christ, and accepts the gift of the indwelling of the Holy Spirit. This process often includes water baptism, which symbolizes the washing away of the old person.

Following the Christian life calls for us to recognize that we are sinners saved by grace. Jesus gave us a way to heal the pain caused by our sin. He modeled what we should do–live a life based on practicing selfless love and caring for the poor and the dispossessed, forgiveness of sin, and nonviolence. We can increase the possibility of living a Christian life through fervent prayer, right conduct toward nonbelievers, not allowing the circumstances of life to make a difference in our spiritual relationships with others, and making all discourse (talk) discreet. As authentic Christians we have a responsibility to strive to realize the Kingdom envisioned by Jesus.

Whenever we search for ways to feel the presence of the Holy Spirit in our inner, worship, or community lives, it is usually a result of the nudging of the new creature we have become since receiving the gift of the Holy Spirit. This gift is given by God to those He has chosen. It is a source of holiness and happiness, and receiving it cures the restlessness that comes from being separated from God. It provides a sense of spiritual, mental, and physical health, regardless of our denominational choices or economic and social positions. As believers we come to realize that we are no longer separated from God. Indeed, nothing can separate us from Him. Christ promised us that even though He would leave us, He would provide "another comforter"—who is the Holy Spirit (see Jn. 16:7). Thereby, we are able to continue our communion with Him in His absence through His presence in the indwelling Holy Spirit.

Regardless of denomination, Christians' questions on how to live a Spirit-filled life are as old as Christianity. Therefore, a variety of persons may find something on the pages of this book that will be helpful in their search for an understanding of what is required on the Christian path.

Finally, it is important for us to recognize that much of life is learned through trial and error. We watch our parents. We go to church and to school. Our friends, and later our mentors, tell us and show us how to think, act, and behave in ways that will make us acceptable to our family, community, and society. The basic principles of the Christian life are learned in much the same way. We have a decided advantage in knowing what to expect, how to act, and to whom we ultimately belong when those who surround us travel the Christian path. Even if we choose a different route for ourselves, the Bible reminds us of the ongoing possibility of returning to our relationship with God: "Train up a child in the way he should go: and when he is old, he will not depart from it" (Prov. 22:6).

If we lack positive role models, often we think we have stumbled upon the Christian path on our own. Yet ultimately, in all cases, the gift of the Holy Spirit is the guide to the Christian path. Whatever the way we find the path, the new creature we become by our repentance, belief, and baptism is worth the price we must pay to follow Jesus, our model for the Christian life.

A note of caution needs to be added here: Salvation is an individual experience. Therefore, children born into Christian families are not saved by virtue of their families' standing with God. Each of us must individually hear the call, become believers, and be baptized.

Living the life of a Christian in whatever time we are born, although filled with challenges, is possible if we build in the necessary supports.

- Study the Scriptures because they point the way.
- Seek and follow the directions of the indwelling Holy Spirit. He always knows what we are to be, what we are to do, and where we are to go. Most importantly, He knows how we are to get there.
- Pray and meditate daily.
- Participate in a community of believers who can help you to sustain yourself in times of brokenness and despair.
- Mentor others and be open to mentoring (discipling) by others.

Chapter 1

Light Afflictions

The "grace of faith" is the remedy against "fainting in times of trouble." New saints are often puzzled about ways to balance the problems (light afflictions) they must face on a daily basis against what Scripture promises (weight of glory) them if they endure (see 2 Cor. 4:17). They may have to withstand being forsaken by their friends, and persecuted by their enemies; but God has promised to never leave or forsake them (see Heb. 13:5). Indeed, His resurrection provides encouragement to endure. Our suffering in this world, with things like racism and other forms of persecution, is small compared to the denial and crucifixion experienced by Christ. It is also a small price to pay for the reward of everlasting life.

We who are God's children are saved by grace through faith in our Lord Jesus Christ, and we are kept by His power. In His care, the life of a Christian is designed to be a life of blessedness, joy, contentment, and kindness. Following the Christian path, we also learn how to genuinely love our brothers and sisters in Christ. It is also important for us to know that we are not provided with divine protection or immunity from the normal circumstances of life. We shall continue to know death, loss, sorrow, and disappointment. As Christians we can anticipate a certain amount of suffering that seems directly related to our profession that we are Christians. Nevertheless, we are expected to endure this suffering without giving up our beliefs.

We can endure whatever comes against us because we know that we will find further comfort in the Lord's promise of a great reward in the end. Jesus said, "Blessed are ye, when men shall revile you, and persecute you, and shall say all manner of evil against you falsely, for My sake. Rejoice, and be exceeding glad: for great is your reward in heaven: for so persecuted they the prophets which were before you" (Mt. 5:11-12). The apostle Paul directly refers to the issue in Second Corinthians 4:17, "For our light affliction, which is but for a moment, worketh for us a far more exceeding and eternal weight of glory." The Bible points out in very clear language that when we suffer and endure for the name of the Lord, we can look forward to a great reward in Heaven.

There are those who criticize Christians for looking toward Heaven for their final reward. Yet final reward will surely come, either in Heaven or in hell. Since death and judgment are inescapable (see Heb. 9:27), we shall take heed to the words of the prophet Amos when he said, "...Prepare to meet thy God..." (Amos 4:12).

Some say that death is a long way off, and therefore, we should prepare ourselves to live and enjoy the life that God has given us. Whether or not death is a long way off is truly unknown. However, I agree that life should be lived to the fullest. We should seek greater education, have ambition, work hard, and enjoy whatever material benefits we earn. As has been indicated, life goes beyond material things. It also reaches out to that which is eternal. This wholeness, the balancing of the demands of the eternal with the demands of the material, when achieved, is the result of living a Spirit-filled life.

I have no doubt of the final, total, and absolute victory of the child of God. Jesus' words in the Scripture are clear on this subject, "My sheep hear My voice, and I know them, and they follow Me: and I give unto them eternal life; and they shall never perish, neither shall any man pluck them out of My hand" (Jn. 10:27-28). Some have said, "Well, no one can pluck you out of His hand, but you can jump out." This cannot be true because Jesus said, "They shall never perish." Jesus' words were not conditional; they were certain. He didn't say, "*If* they hear My voice." He didn't say, "*If* they follow Me." He said, "My sheep *hear* My voice, and they follow Me and they shall *never* perish."

Chapter 2

Security of the Saints

As Christians we are told that we are to endure to the end. This endurance is to be undertaken in spite of the fact that we shall be hated of all men for the sake of Jesus because "...he that shall endure unto the end, the same shall be saved" (Mk. 13:13). In essence, endurance is possible in all circumstances because our needs will be supplied.

Some will contradict this statement, saying that they have known people whose needs were not supplied and who, consequently, turned back and were lost. I base my position on the security of the saints upon the Word of God. When there appear to be contradictions in Scripture, our lack of knowledge is usually the source of the error.

The writers of the Bible, the blueprint of our faith, wrote as they were inspired to by God. Without this divine inspiration, we must rely completely on our human experience. Human experience is subjective.

Consequently, one person may feel one way and another may feel something entirely different. The Bible teaches us that as children of God we will be victorious over all opposition because we are in the hands of the Father.

In Matthew 6:31-33, Jesus says,

> *Therefore take no thought, saying, What shall we eat? or, What shall we drink? or Wherewithal shall we be clothed? (For after all these things do the Gentiles seek:) for your heavenly Father knoweth that ye have need of all these things. But seek ye first the kingdom of God, and His righteousness; and all these things shall be added unto you.*

I am convinced that just as God tells us He is going to meet all of our needs materially (with shoes, clothes, and food), He tells us just as certainly that He is going to meet all of our needs spiritually.

In Philippians 4:12-13, the apostle Paul writes,

> *I know both how to be abased, and I know how to abound: every where and in all things I am instructed both to be full and to be hungry, both to abound and to suffer need. I can do all things through Christ which strengtheneth me.*

What is Paul saying here? He is saying that no situation, material or spiritual, will be too difficult because we can do all things through faith in Christ.

One may ask, "Why are you so positive? Aren't you being a bit presumptuous?" No! It is not presumptuous to believe the Word of God. When we raise our voices to sing such words as, "My hope is built on nothing less than Jesus' blood and righteousness," we must believe what we are singing. If we don't believe the words of the songs we sing, then we should not sing them. The assurance we have of salvation is based upon the fact that we believe the Bible to be right when it tells us we were chosen and predestined to be conformed to the image of His Son and to be adopted as children by Jesus Christ to Himself according to the good pleasure of His will (see Eph. 1:4-5; Rom. 8:29). We can rest secure in the knowledge that He who began, "...a good work in you will perform it..." (Phil. 1:6).

The God of the Old and New Testaments is not a helpless, powerless deity who has lost control and cannot save us or keep us saved unless we allow Him to do so. That is the picture many people have of God. They see a God who is desperately trying to save humankind, but is powerless to do so without the permission of those He so passionately wants to save. I have heard it said many times that God cannot save you if you do not want to be saved and that God cannot keep you if you do not want to be kept. This position effectively makes us, the creature, stronger than God, the Creator. This is not to say that God will drag us into Heaven kicking and screaming, "I don't want to go to Heaven, Lord," while God says, "You are going to go whether you like it or not."

The God of the Bible, the God we know, is the God who met a miserable creature like Saul of Tarsus on the

Damascus Road. We can read in the Bible the history of Saul of Tarsus. This man not only did not want to be saved, but he thought that he was already saved. He hated the name of Jesus. God stopped him on the road to Damascus and changed his mind completely. He became known as Paul, the greatest Christian missionary the world has ever known. God made the change. God saved Paul; and not because his heart was all that good (although he was not a bad man as far as the law was concerned). He was, however, an enemy of the Church and was threatening to slaughter it.

Some will say, "Paul persecuted the Church in ignorance." This is true. However, natural law tells us that ignorance does not alter the consequences of an action. If we drink carbolic acid thinking it is 7 Up, we will die. If a mother, while making a cake, accidentally puts rat poison into the ingredients, believing it to be flour, and feeds it to her children, they will die. We cannot escape the consequences by saying, I didn't know. Why? Because these are poisons. If you back off a ten-story building, you will fall to the ground even if you didn't realize what you were doing. God's spiritual laws are just as constant as His natural laws. "The soul that sinneth, it shall die..." (Ezek. 18:20). Without God's intervention, we could never make it to Heaven.

Let us examine some examples of God's power to intervene. These passages record Israel's experience in Egypt:

> *Else, if thou wilt not let My people go, behold, I will send swarms of flies upon thee, and upon thy servants,*

and upon thy people, and into thy houses: and the houses of the Egyptians shall be full of swarms of flies, and also the ground whereon they are. And I will sever in that day the land of Goshen, in which My people dwell, that no swarms of flies shall be there (Exodus 8:21-22a).

...Moses stretched forth his rod toward heaven: and the Lord sent thunder and hail, and the fire ran along upon the ground; and the Lord rained hail upon the land of Egypt. So there was hail, and fire mingled with the hail, very grievous, such as there was none like it in all the land of Egypt since it became a nation. And the hail smote throughout all the land of Egypt all that was in the field, both man and beast; and the hail smote every herb of the field, and brake every tree of the field. Only in the land of Goshen, where the children of Israel were, was there no hail (Exodus 9:23-26).

Chapter 3

God Is Sovereign

The Bible is a witness to God's sovereignty, to His supreme, or absolute, power. It is a witness to His ability to allow certain things to happen. In Exodus 10:21-23, the Word of God tells us,

> *And the Lord said unto Moses, Stretch out thine hand toward heaven, that there may be darkness over the land of Egypt, even darkness which may be felt. And Moses stretched forth his hand toward heaven; and there was a thick darkness in all the land of Egypt three days: they saw not one another, neither rose any from his place for three days: but all the children of Israel had light in their dwellings.*

Other examples of God's power can be seen in Exodus 12:13 and Daniel 3:23-25. Exodus reports that throughout all Egypt, the firstborn would die except in the houses of Israel, where the lamb had been slain and blood had been placed over the door posts. The Lord said, "...when I see the blood, I will pass over you...."

Daniel tells of the Hebrew boys who were cast into the fiery furnace. Hands bound, they said they would not bow down to the idol. So they were cast into the fiery furnace. But what do we see in this passage? We see them liberated in the fire. Their bonds were broken, and they were seen walking on the fiery coals, and it was said, "Look, didn't we cast three in? There are four, and the fourth one looks like the Son of God."

The story of the Hebrew boys indicates that the Lord does not always deliver us from the fire; sometimes we have to go through it. Yet we have an assurance that while we're in the fire, the Lord will be walking along right beside us. Sometimes, the Lord has to take us through something in order to free us from some of the things that bind us. There have been and will be times when we will have wrong ideas. No one will be able to change them or talk to us about them. Even reading the Bible will seem fruitless. In times like these the Lord may take us through the fires of suffering, trial, or difficulty. The fire of suffering often liberates us.

The power of God is all encompassing, and this power does all things. Jesus had power over the sea and the wind. In the storm, His disciples asked Him, "Master, carest Thou not that we perish?" (Mk. 4:38b) Jesus spoke to the winds and the waves. The winds stopped blowing and the waves subsided. God has power over nature. The One who can say to the wind, "Stop blowing," the One who can say to the waves, "Peace, be still," can certainly keep us in our hour of trial. In times of trial we must remember that He is the same One who caused the flies to sweep over Egypt, yet His people were free from them. He is the One who caused a darkness so thick that the people of Egypt could not move out of their houses or see one another. Yet in the houses of His people there was light. He is the same One who caused hail to break down trees and destroy all the harvest and corn in Egypt, yet in the land of Goshen there was no hail.

Why do we not trust God more? How can we look at "so great a cloud of witnesses" (Heb. 12:1) and then see God as someone who can't do anything unless we allow Him to do it?

Chapter 4

Saved by Grace

The foundation of the security spoken of by Peter, Paul, and the other apostles is God's choice for His people. This choice was based on "free grace" because the choice was made before the creation of the universe. In other words, grace is a gift from God. Paul's letter to the Ephesians validates this:

> *Blessed be the God and Father of our Lord Jesus Christ, who hath blessed us with all spiritual blessings in heavenly places in Christ: according as He hath chosen us in Him before the foundation of the world, that we should be holy and without blame before Him in love: having predestinated us unto the adoption of children by Jesus Christ to Himself…"* (Ephesians 1:3-5).

What a mighty God we serve! He made His choice before we were born. Now, having chosen us, do you think He is going to let the devil take us back? God has declared the end from the beginning, saying, "My counsel shall stand, and I will do all My pleasure" (Is. 46:10b).

The security of the saints is reinforced in the Scripture that reminds us: "...greater is He that is in you, than he that is in the world" (1 Jn. 4:4). New believers have many concerns about situations that could cause them to be lost. One such concern is demon possession. This ceases to be an issue for children of God because the Scriptures tell us that the Lord casts out demons.

God knows all things. God knew what we would do before He saved us. He knew He would save us before we knew we were going to be saved. Some people think that God doesn't know everything. I read some Sunday School literature in which a commentator stated that God knows everything except what people will do under stress. This view holds that God can only know what is knowable and that what we will do under stress is not knowable until it is done. This view strips God of His omniscience. If God doesn't know what we will do under stress and must wait until we do it to have knowledge of it, not only does God not know everything, God is ever learning from us. This is not the God that we know. As a matter of fact, this view of God takes us far from what is written in the Bible.

Chapter 5

Why Pray?

If God knows everything, why pray? A primary reason for praying is because the Bible tells us to. First Thessalonians 5:17, a very short verse, says, "Pray without ceasing." In Luke 18:1 we are told, "And He spake a parable unto them to this end, that men ought always to pray, and not to faint." In James 5:15-16 we learn,

> *And the prayer of faith shall save the sick, and the Lord shall raise him up; and if he have committed sins, they shall be forgiven him. Confess your faults one to another, and pray one for another, that ye may be healed. The effectual fervent prayer of a righteous man availeth much.*

The apostle Paul also addresses the issue of the importance of prayer when he writes:

> *Likewise the Spirit also helpeth our infirmities: for we know not what we should pray for as we ought: but the*

Spirit Itself maketh intercession for us with groanings which cannot be uttered. And He that searcheth the hearts knoweth what is the mind of the Spirit, because He maketh intercession for the saints according to the will of God (Romans 8:26-27).

Paul knew how to pray, yet he implies that he does not know how he ought to pray. What does this mean for us? As Christians, old and new, we have many frailties and failings that would overpower us if we were left to ourselves. Therefore, the Holy Spirit teaches us what to pray for. He works within us to calm our fears, and to help us to overcome disappointments. The Holy Spirit knows all we desire of God, which is often more than words can utter. Consequently, He searches our hearts, perceives our minds, and makes intercession to God on our behalf. When we pray we are communicating with One who knows not only what we tell Him, but also that of which we are not consciously aware (the sincerity of the prayer; what is really in our heart of hearts). When we pray, it is actually God Himself, the indwelling Spirit (God present), that inspires us to do so. It is something in us that is not of ourselves that intercedes for us before God. It is strange and mysterious to think about God in us praying to Himself. Yet who better knows the deep things buried in our souls?

So, when a person asks "Why should we pray?" our first response can be: Scripture instructs us to do so. Our second response can be: It brings the deeper levels of our being, of which we are not aware, before God, and ultimately, it brings these levels into our own awareness. The power and meaning of prayer are found in the act of God working through us to raise our whole being to Him.

Prayer is a means to an end. Let me give you a simplified example. If you want to travel from a certain place to New York, you don't get to New York by just saying, "I am in New York." To get to New York, you must do something. There are means by which you can accomplish the goal. You either drive, take a train, a plane, or walk. Prayer is one way through which God leads us to what He wants us to know and where He wants us to go. The Bible says He knows what is needed and wanted before you even ask Him (see Mt. 6:8).

There are two kinds of prayers: *formulated prayers*, those that are sometimes mechanical, and *spontaneous prayers*, ordinary conversations with someone who is called God. Within these categories are prayers in which we beg or request, prayers of intercession (prayers on behalf of others), prayers of confession, and prayers of praise. It matters not what kind of prayer we pray, nor does it matter if we cannot find the "right" words. What matters is that God is able to search our hearts, and He knows and hears regardless of our ability to use the "right" words.

Chapter 6

Not of Ourselves: The New Birth

Insomuch as the Bible teaches we are "dead in trespasses and sins" (Eph. 2:1), how does one come into an awareness of God, and exhibit the vital signs of spiritual life? The answer to that question can be found in the words of Jesus to Nicodemus, "Verily, verily, I say unto thee, Except a man be born again, he cannot see the kingdom of God" (Jn. 3:3b). We have already been born. We were born after the flesh. Now we are born again. The means by which this change takes place is the Word of God. The Scriptures say, "...Faith cometh by hearing, and hearing by the word of God" (Rom. 10:17).

Another passage spells out the role of the Word of God in the plan of salvation: "Being born again, not of corruptible seed, but of incorruptible, by the word of God, which liveth and abideth for ever" (1 Pet. 1:23). It is through the Word of God that we responded to the truth. "Whereby are given unto us exceeding great and precious promises: that by these ye might be partakers of the divine nature, having escaped the corruption that is in the world through lust" (2 Pet. 1:4). The divine promises of God have come to us through the Word of God.

Since birth is the beginning of natural life, being born anew, or "from above," is the beginning of a spiritual life. Patching up the old nature by remorse and reformation, accompanied by resolutions and promises to amend one's life, is not sufficient. There must be a new life characterized by new values, new principles of living, and new aims and directions. In the first birth we were shaped in iniquity and conceived in sin (see Ps. 51:5). Paul described the condition of human sin when he wrote, "There is none righteous, no, not one" (Rom. 3:10b). Paul further described humanity's corrupt and depraved state, "...the carnal mind is enmity against God: for it is not subject to the law of God, neither indeed can be. So then they that are in the flesh cannot please God" (Rom. 8:7-8). Hence, one must be "born again." The theological term for this act is *regeneration.*

The birth of a human being is considered by many to be the "miracle of life." Birth is a natural act, which is usually preceded by a nine-month period of gestation. It ends with the emergence of a new human being into the world—a new soul coming into existence. Another act, which is even more miraculous, is the new birth of a sinner, for by that new birth that person becomes a child of God. This is not a natural act, but a supernatural one. It is an act accomplished by God Himself.

In a natural birth, certain things take place prior to the actual birth. The baby to-be begins as just one small speck; then it grows and develops into an embryo. The embryo develops into a fetus, and eventually it becomes the newborn infant we see in the delivery room. So it is with being born again. Although there are many stages in this process, at this time I am concerned with three: hearing the Word preached (or being taught), making a decision, and conversion. We are all familiar with hearing the Word preached or taught. Therefore, we shall move directly to discussing conversion. Conversion is the act of the individual turning toward God. It means a person has turned, or changed his or her course, and based upon certain decisions he or she has made, is now moving toward God.

The new birth process is under the control of God because the act of conversion, or making a decision for Christ, cannot be done without the aid of God Himself. One cannot do it alone. This is confirmed by the words of Jesus, "No man can come to Me, except the Father which hath sent Me draw him: and I will raise him up at the last day" (Jn. 6:44). Jesus made it very clear that in order for one to come to Him, he or she must have the help of God. Any time a person turns toward God, any time a person looks toward holiness and sanctification, it is an absolute indication that God is dealing with that individual. God does not just deal with the individual after he turns to Him; God is the *reason* the individual turns to Him.

Some people think the decision to turn to God was their own, unaided decision. They think God reached out to them after their initial decision to receive Him. You know the old saying, "If you make the first step, God will make two." In human terms that sounds reasonable, but in spiritual terms you cannot make the first step unless there is a divine, motivating presence.

The Scripture tells us that God is, in fact, the determining factor in our turning to Him.

> *But as many as received Him, to them gave He power to become the sons of God, even to them that believe on His name: which were born, not of blood, nor of the will of the flesh, nor of the will of man, but of God* (John 1:12-13).

In the natural birth we were born by the human will. But, in the spiritual birth, we are born of God.

James 1:18 tells us, "Of His own will begat He us with the word of truth, that we should be a kind of firstfruits of His creatures." Of His own will, not of our will, "begat He us." There are countless thousands who have not understood the blessed truth: God is the "first cause" in salvation and that it is He who saved us, and not we ourselves (see Ps. 100:3).

The Scripture says,

> *...The carnal mind is enmity against God: for it is not subject to the law of God, neither indeed can be. So*

then they that are in the flesh cannot please God. But ye are not in the flesh, but in the Spirit, if so be that the Spirit of God dwell in you. Now if any man have not the Spirit of Christ, he is none of His" (Romans 8:7-9).

What is the state of our unreformed nature? It is death. Death is a state of separation; thus, the sinner is in a state of separation from God as is seen in the following Scripture:

And you hath He quickened, who were dead in trespasses and sins; wherein in time past ye walked according to the course of this world, according to the prince of the power of the air, the spirit that now worketh in the children of disobedience: among whom also we all had our conversation in times past in the lusts of our flesh, fulfilling the desires of the flesh and of the mind; and were by nature the children of wrath, even as others. But God, who is rich in mercy, for His great love wherewith He loved us, even when we were dead in sins, hath quickened us together with Christ, (by grace ye are saved) (Ephesians 2:1-5).

This passage from Paul's letter to the Ephesians is proof that God is the initiator of our salvation, not we ourselves. The evidence is overwhelming that deliverance from the enslavement of sin cannot be accomplished by the individual unaided by the Holy Ghost. Our sinful nature is so marred and impaired that the Bible refers to that state of being as "dead in trespasses and in sins." The Scripture teaches us that there is none who is good, no, not one (Rom. 3:12).

Chapter 7

Union With Christ

There is another aspect of being born again. It is referred to as a *union with Christ.* It is one of the great truths taught in the Bible, yet it is also one of the most neglected truths because so few Christians know of it. A.W. Pink, one of today's greatest theologians, commented,

> "The subject of spiritual union is the most important, the most profound and yet the most blessed of any that is set forth in the sacred Scripture. And yet, sad to say, there is hardly any which is now more generally neglected. The very expression of spiritual union is unknown in most professing Christian circles and even where it is employed, it is given such a protracted meaning as to take in only a fragment of this precious truth."[1]

---

1. Arthur W. Pink, *Spiritual Union and Communion* (Grand Rapids, MI: Baker Publishing, 1971), 7.

Pink felt the concept of union with Christ was totally ignored in many Christian churches. But this aspect of the new birth, if properly understood, will be of great value to the child of God. Jesus gave many illustrations of this. One such illustration is found in John 15:1,4-5:

> *I am the true vine, and My Father is the husbandman. ... Abide in Me, and I in you. As the branch cannot bear fruit of itself, except it abide in the vine; no more can ye, except ye abide in Me. I am the vine, ye are the branches: He that abideth in Me, and I in him, the same bringeth forth much fruit: for without Me ye can do nothing.*

If we are united in Christ through the indwelling of the Holy Spirit, we will produce the fruits of the Spirit. Furthermore, just as a branch withers without the life-giving substance that flows from the vine, we will not be able to produce fruit if we are cut off from Christ.

Union with Christ doesn't come automatically. It comes by being filled, or being baptized, with the Holy Spirit. In First Corinthians 12:13 Paul writes, "For by one Spirit are we all baptized into one body, whether we be Jews or Gentiles, whether we be bond or free; and have been all made to drink into one Spirit."

In Romans 8:9, Paul demonstrates this union with Christ in another way: "But ye are not in the flesh, but in the Spirit, if so be that the Spirit of God dwell in you. Now if any man have not the Spirit of Christ, he is none of His." Compare what is said in verse 8 with verse 9: "So then they that are in the flesh cannot please God"; "But ye are not in the flesh, but in the Spirit, if so be that the Spirit of God dwell in you...."

Chapter 8

Sacramentarianism

Many believe that they are saved through the sacraments. Sacraments are described as outward and visible signs ordained by Christ, setting forth and pledging an inward and spiritual blessing[1] Being baptized in water, taking communion, reciting catechisms, going to church, saying prayers, and taking instructions are examples of sacraments. However, none of these are the same as being "born again." Many people think that they are saved because they do these things. Let me swiftly add that all born-again Christians do these things, but doing them, of themselves, does not signify that the new birth has taken place.

The use of sacraments is called sacramentarianism. Sacramentarians rarely talk about being saved. They talk about being a Christian. There is nothing wrong

1. *Illustrated Bible Dictionary*, Vol. 3 (Wheaton, IL: Tyndale House Publishers, 1986), 1357.

with being a Christian. Praise the Lord, I am a Christian. But being a Christian and being saved are different. If you were born in a Christian country and were raised in a Christian family, although you might not go to church, if you were asked about your religion, you would, in all probability, say that you are a Christian. The term *Christian* is often used in its broadest sense to describe a religious belief, culture, or tradition. Consequently, when a person says that he or she is a Christian, it does not always follow that the declaration of being a Christian is synonymous with being "born again."

Heredity and the environment do not signify the new birth. Therefore, being born into a home where your parents are saved does not mean that you are saved. Salvation is not hereditary. It cannot be passed on through the genes from one generation to the next.

I would say that people who are born in Christian homes and who are brought up in a nurturing environment have an advantage, but that is not the new birth. Going to church, learning catechisms, attending new members classes and having one's name placed on the church roll does not indicate that a person has been regenerated or born again. It may mean that you are a Christian in the general sense of the word, but it doesn't mean that you are saved.

Some will take issue with me on this concept of the new birth, but Christ defined it when He said, "I am the way, the truth, and the life" (Jn. 14:6). He, who said,

"...the words that I speak unto you, they are spirit, and they are life" (Jn. 6:63) is the same who said, "...Ye must be born again" (Jn. 3:7).

Chapter 9

Sanctification

The new birth is both instantaneous and progressive. When we are born again, we are immediately sanctified and justified. However, there is a shade of difference between sanctification and justification. The word *sanctified* comes from the Greek word *hagiasmos*, which generally means "to be set apart." So when we are saved, we are set apart by God. This "setting apart" doesn't mean that we have achieved perfection. It means that we are now different. As Jesus said, "They are not of the world, even as I am not of the world" (Jn. 17:16). The progressiveness of sanctification is seen in the fact that the longer we are saved and under the influence of the Holy Spirit, the more set apart we become. We are that much further from the world, from its scheming and plotting, and from the habits we developed while in the world.

When we are newly saved we bring with us some heavy baggage, like bad habits. Some of these habits vanish overnight; others cling like hungry leeches. But as we make progress in God, we begin to shake these habits. This is progressing in Christ, being more sanctified or set apart. We should be closer to God five years after being saved than five months after being saved.

Chapter 10

Living Holy

The Lord chose us for salvation. However, just because He chose us does not mean we are going to Heaven while we continue in our sin. There is a means by which we get to Heaven. What is that means? Holiness. We are set apart by God to do the service of God through prayer, repentance of our sins, being born again, and charitable works. In essence, we live a godly life. The Bible tells us to "Follow peace with all men, and holiness, without which no man shall see the Lord" (Heb. 12:14). Holiness provides the means by which God takes us from earth to glory.

Therefore, when we talk about being saved by grace, it should not be assumed that we will continue to sin. That is why it is so important for those of us who claim to be saved to live as one who has "risen with Christ." We want to live in harmony with Christ's teachings because that is the mark of a born-again child of God. Jesus said, "Ye shall know them by their fruits.... A good tree cannot bring forth evil fruit, neither can a corrupt tree bring forth good fruit" (Mt. 7:16,18).

God has a specific end for us, and He has a means to bring us to that end. There are those who will ask how we can be so sure that God can succeed since it appears that God has had to change from time to time. There are some passages in the Bible, if taken out of context, that give the appearance that God has made mistakes and been sorry about them. If, however, we read these passages in the light of the teaching of the whole Bible, we can easily see that this is not the case. Let's look at a few examples.

"And it repented the Lord that He had made man on the earth, and it grieved Him at His heart" (Gen. 6:6). Here it appears that God was sorry that He had created humans because He didn't know that they would sin. Another passage reads, "And the Lord said, Because the cry of Sodom and Gomorrah is great, and because their sin is very grievous; I will go down now, and see whether they have done altogether according to the cry of it, which is come unto Me; and if not, I will know" (Gen. 18:20-21). In Genesis 22:12, the Lord speaks to Abraham after preventing him from offering his son as a sacrifice, "...Lay not thine hand upon the lad, neither do thou any thing unto him: for now I know that thou fearest God, seeing thou hast not withheld thy son, thine only son from Me."

The above passages can give the impression that God did not know certain things beforehand. Statements like these are *anthropomorphic*. This word is taken from two Greek words, *anthropos* meaning man and *morphe* meaning form. Anthropomorphism is something manlike. The Bible is written to men, and it is written in manlike terms. You will find an example of this in Joshua 10:12-13.

> *Then spake Joshua to the Lord in the day when the Lord delivered up the Amorites before the children of Israel, and he said in the sight of Israel, Sun, stand thou still upon Gibeon; and thou, Moon, in the valley of Aijalon. And the sun stood still....*

The earth is the moving sphere, revolving on its own axis. However, to men it appears as if the sun rises and sets. The men of Joshua's day did not know that, so Joshua, using his own understanding, commanded the sun to stand still. This is an anthropomorphism. (Please note that the intent here is not to be chauvinistic, but to define a word in its historical context. Therefore in this context, manlike also includes womanlike or humanlike behavior without regard to gender.)

Another example of an anthropomorphism is found in Revelation 7:1, "And after these things I saw four angels standing on the four corners of the earth...." Now we know the earth doesn't have four corners because the earth is round. However, historically men thought the earth was flat.

In summary, no one with an understanding of Scripture and the nature of God can think of God as being repentant or unknowing. The word *repent*, in its strictest sense means to have a change of mind. We know, however, that God spoke to the prophet Malachi and said, "For I am the Lord, I change not..." (Mal. 3:6). The Scripture also says, "God is not a man, that He should lie; neither the son of man, that He should repent" (Num. 23:19a).

God, who is infinite in majesty and in whose hands all things reside, in unfolding His eternal purposes inspired the Bible writers to write in the everyday language of the people, and they often described things as they appeared to be, not necessarily as they really were.

Chapter 11

Justification

Justification is instantaneous, and it means that God begins to look upon each of us as a person who has never committed a single sin. Although we committed many sins before being saved, afterward in the mind of God all those sins are totally abolished. Our sins may not be totally abolished in our minds because some of us have done things that may still bother us, and our consciences may make us feel guilty. We don't have enough faith to believe God has truly washed them all away. Let's look more closely at an example of justification from an event that may occur in the natural course of things:

If a person kills an intruder who has broken into his or her home, under normal circumstances when the police arrive, they will arrest the person. Even though the doors may have been broken down or the windows broken out, the police will arrest the person, and he or she will undoubtedly go to jail for a time. But, if in the due process of law it is decided that the person who killed the intruder did so in defense of his or her life, that is not called murder, but justifiable homicide. Once this decision is made, the jail doors open and the person walks out and stands in society as if he or she had never committed the act. There was no trial by jury, and no prison term was warranted because the judge ruled the act as justified. The person is exonerated from the guilt of murder. And, the person cannot be more justified 25 years later than he or she was on the first day of the judge's ruling.

Another example that might clarify the concept of justification is the birth of a child. A child can never be more born when he or she is 50 years old than when he or she is one minute old.

For further reading on the subjects of sanctification and justification, see the writings of the apostles Paul and John. Both of these men also expounded on the union with Christ. In addition, Paul's writings address election, predestination, and righteousness, while John's address the new birth, or the born-again experience.

Chapter 12

The Sinful Nature

As we study this important doctrine of new birth, it is very important to keep in mind that in the born-again experience the sinful nature is broken, but not totally abolished. The child of God no longer lives under sin's dominance, but the sinful nature is still present. Some people wonder why they still have unhealthy, worldly feelings and desires after they are saved. Sometimes they are tempted to do things they really don't want to do, and they are confused because they thought these temptations would be a thing of the past. They thought their sinful nature was gone, but it was not. We carry our sinful nature with us until we draw our last breath because it is our human nature, and our human nature is ruined, degraded, and sinful. The depravity of human nature is the result of Adam's fall, and we have all inherited Adam's fallen nature. Our civilization and culture lead us to believe that we are not so bad. However, in order to protect ourselves from our own sinful inclinations, we have constructed a body of laws, customs, and mores to govern our behavior. This is why we have city councils, state legislatures, a congress, and so forth. They make laws that the police, the judges, and prisons enforce.

The point I am making is that sinful men and women need to be regenerated, or changed, radically for the better. This process ends their domination by their old selves. In Romans 6:14-16, we read,

> *For sin shall not have dominion over you: for ye are not under the law, but under grace. What then? shall we sin, because we are not under the law, but under grace? God forbid. Know ye not, that to whom ye yield yourselves servants to obey, his servants ye are to whom ye obey; whether of sin unto death, or of obedience unto righteousness? But God be thanked, that ye were the servants of sin, but ye have obeyed from the heart that form of doctrine which was delivered you. Being then made free from sin, ye became the servants of righteousness.*

The word *servant* used here does not convey Paul's true thought. The word *servant* is taken from the Greek word *doulos*. It means to be a bond slave, not an indentured slave. An indentured slave was one who was in slavery working out a debt. A bond slave was a person that someone owned. No one wants to be a slave to another human being, but to be a slave for Christ, to be a slave in the hands of God is a different matter all together. Jesus said that no man can serve two masters (see Lk. 16:13). Consequently, when the individual is freed from the dominion of sin, he is freed from the dominion of his sinful nature. This enables the child of God to live a consistent life of righteousness. This, however, does not mean that a person is then sinlessly perfect.

I know there are those who insist that a person can be absolutely sinless. Many of us have often heard the statement made, "You must make 100 percent; 99 percent won't do." How many people do you know who are 100 percent loving, 100 percent unselfish, 100 percent kind, 100 percent pure, or 100 percent giving? The moment a healthy person calls his employer to inform him or her that he or she is ill and will not be in for work, that 100 percent purity goes out the window. Any shading of the truth, any wrong motives, any half truths, such as envy, strife, covetousness, or backbiting, mars the sinless image. It is true that a person may feel 100 percent perfect because his or her life is not scarred by sexual immorality, drunkenness, and other gross sins and vices, but that life is not sinlessly pure.

Do Christians commit sin? Unfortunately, the answer is "yes." Some honest, but misguided, ministers deny the fact of sin in the life of the believer on the grounds that to admit to such a thing would be catering to weakness. Telling the truth is not catering to weakness. The Bible says that if a man says he has no sin, the truth is not in him (see 1 Jn. 1:8). However, sin is something that should rarely occur in a Christian's life. It is not something that should happen all the time. A Christian does not continue in sin. The child of God does not make a practice of it. He or she doesn't sin willingly.

Chapter 13

The Remedy

The following Scripture points out the remedy for sin in the life of a Christian: "...If we walk in the light, as He is in the light, we have fellowship one with another, and the blood of Jesus Christ His Son cleanseth us from all sin" (1 Jn. 1:7). Greek scholars tell us that this verse is written in the continuating tense, so it can be read, "If we are walking in the light as He is in the light, the blood of Jesus Christ His Son continually cleanses us from all sin."

As Christians we are in need of the cleansing blood of Christ throughout our lives. John writes in the next verse, "If we say that we have no sin, we deceive ourselves, and truth is not in us" (1 Jn. 1:8). You will notice that John is writing to the Church. He did not write, "If *they* say," but "If *we* say." He further writes, "If we confess our sins, He is faithful and just to forgive us our sins, and to cleanse us from all unrighteousness" (1 Jn. 1:9).

So being freed from the domination of sin does not speak to perfection, but it speaks to the fact that we are not living the kind of sinful life that we lived before being saved. We have another life now. We have been born again and the old life is behind us. Anyone who claims to be indwelt by the Holy Spirit and still clings to the old sinful lifestyle, has never been born again. This is not to say that a true Christian does not have problems. The Scriptures, as well as life experience, give witness to the fact that Christians must deal with sin in their lives. Nevertheless, having been born again, the believer is no longer subject to the dominance of his or her sinful nature.

Being born again changes our relationship with God to the extent that it is similar to being raised from the dead and being delivered from a life of total alienation. The believer is not, however, delivered from all the temptations and pitfalls that are present in the life of a Christian. Too often Christians think they are immune from disappointment and failure. Certain ministers in churches, on radio, and television lead people to believe that God will answer every prayer in the affirmative no matter how unreasonable or selfish it may be.

These ministers seem to think that the only reason for God's existence is to give us what we want. They tell us to ask for what we want, claim it, and if we ask in Jesus' name and have faith, God will give it to us. There is no suffering in their vocabulary. There is no self-denial in their vocabulary. There is nothing about God's will in their vocabulary. It is entirely about what we want and nothing else. God, they say, must give us our request, and if we don't get it there is something wrong with us.

Where is God in this scenario? Does God have a will? Does God have a purpose for us? Is God just sitting up in Heaven waiting for us to call on Him? Is God nothing more than a celestial bellhop? Is He nothing more than a celestial fireman? Certainly not! God has a plan and a program for each one of us. He, who has the power to guide human destiny, is a kind and loving Father. He knows that although we may want a certain thing we should not have it. Therefore, He will withhold from us.

Most of the time, the things we ask God for we receive. I praise the Lord for that. But sometimes the Lord says, "No." Sometimes the Lord closes the door. And although it may hurt when the Lord closes the door, we should develop the kind of faith that says, "Lord, I know I want such and such, and I don't understand why I am not getting it. However, I know You love me. I know I am Your child, and I know if it were in my best interest, You would give it to me. So, I say, Thy will be done." We must learn how to suffer some things, for, "If we suffer, we shall also reign with Him..." (2 Tim. 2:12).

Chapter 14

The Word of God

It is through the Word of God that we receive our spiritual strength. In Ephesians 6:10-17, Paul likens the weaponry of a Christian to that of the armor of a Roman soldier. Those who have seen pictures of Roman soldiers have seen them equipped with armor, helmets, and shields. Paul tells us to take on the whole armor of God. He talks about having our loins gird with truth, having on the breastplate of righteousness, and having our feet shod with the preparation of the gospel of peace (see Eph. 6:14-15). He talks about the shield of faith and the helmet of salvation. Then in Ephesians 6:17 he says that we should take "the sword of the Spirit, which is the word of God." This is very important. Always keep it before you. It is through the Word of God that we prosper.

We also have the words of the author of the Epistle to the Hebrews:

For the word of God is quick, and powerful, and sharper than any twoedged sword, piercing even to the dividing asunder of soul and spirit, and of the joints and marrow, and is a discerner of the thoughts and intents of the heart (Hebrews 4:12).

We see that the Word of God is not a dead word. The Word of God is not like the Latin language, dead and unchanging. The Word of God is alive. The Word of God is sharp. The Word of God is able to pierce through all the false philosophies that are in the world today.

The Word of God is a means by which we are born again, but this change in us is the work of God. I don't want anyone to get the false impression that if one reads the Word of God and accepts it, that person can be spiritually reborn because of something he or she read in the Bible. God is the author and finisher of our faith (see Heb. 12:2).

Chapter 15

God's Mighty Power

Paul, in his letter to the Ephesians, said that in his prayers he prayed that the saints would know the greatness of God's mighty power. He then compared the greatness of God's power with the power it took to raise Christ from the dead.

> *The eyes of your understanding being enlightened; that ye may know what is the hope of His calling, and what the riches of the glory of His inheritance in the saints, and what is the exceeding greatness of His power to usward who believe, according to the working of His mighty power, which He wrought in Christ, when He raised Him from the dead...* (Ephesians 1:18-20).

I have often wondered if born-again Christians realize that the same power it took to raise Christ from the dead was the same power God utilized to bring the universe into creation. The power that raised Christ from the dead is the same power that is working in us. So don't sell yourself short. Don't view yourself as a pitifully weak saint clinging to salvation, hoping against hope that someday, somehow you'll make it to Heaven. Don't hold yourself in such low esteem, but understand the power that is working in you.

Chapter 16

Ye Must Be Born Again

Since change cannot occur through reformation or reinvigoration, something else must happen, and Jesus made it very clear what that something else is when He said to Nicodemus, "Ye must be born again" (Jn. 3:7b). We have already been born. We were each born after the flesh. We were born after Adam's posterity. Now we must be born again. The means by which this change takes place is the Word of God. Scripture says, "So then faith cometh by hearing, and hearing by the word of God" (Rom. 10:17). There is another passage that spells out the role of the Word of God in the plan of salvation: "Being born again, not of corruptible seed, but of incorruptible, by the word of God, which liveth and abideth for ever" (1 Pet. 1:23). It is through the Word of God that we responded to the truth: "Whereby are given unto us exceeding great and precious promises: that by these ye might be partakers of the divine nature, having escaped the corruption that is in the world through lust" (2 Pet. 1:4). The divine promises of God have come to us through the Word of God.

This salvation is ours only by the grace of God. We cannot pardon our own sins, and no amount of meritorious works can earn us eternal life. A lot of us can't accept this simple truth. Even though it is written in clear language, we seem to feel that acceptance of salvation by grace is a denial of the importance of good works, but this is not so. Grace and good works are not mutually exclusive; they only need to be given their proper place. We are saved by grace and grace alone. Good works are the result of salvation. Scripture tells us,

> *For by grace are ye saved through faith; and that not of yourselves: it is the gift of God: not of works, lest any man should boast. For we are His workmanship, created in Christ Jesus unto good works, which God hath before ordained that we should walk in them* (Ephesians 2:8-10).

Chapter 17

Except the Lord Builds the House

We are not our workmanship, but we are His workmanship. It is God who is conforming us into the image of Christ, and not we ourselves. Not only that, but it is God who causes churches to prosper. We who are ministers make a serious mistake if we think our churches are prospering because we are in beautiful buildings, have fantastic choirs, or have great musicians, or that our oratory causes people to receive Christ. That is the worst mistake we can make. The Bible is very clear on this point, "Except the Lord build the house, they labour in vain that build it: except the Lord keep the city, the watchman waketh but in vain" (Ps. 127:1).

You don't need to have a beautiful church or an excellent choir to grow, nor does the minister have to be a great orator. Why? Because it is not oratory that saves, it is God. This fact can be clearly seen in Paul's letter to the Corinthians.

> *Who then is Paul, and who is Apollos, but ministers by whom ye believed, even as the Lord gave to every man? I have planted, Apollos watered; but God gave the increase. So then neither is he that planteth any thing, neither he that watereth; but God that giveth the increase* (1 Corinthians 3:5-7).

Salvation is the work of God, and we cannot overemphasize that we cannot save ourselves by our good deeds. Good deeds are welcome. Good deeds are things that ought to be done, but they cannot overcome our natural instincts toward sin. I think it was Augustus Strong who wrote that trying to be saved by good deeds is like trying to go south while riding a train going north.

Chapter 18

The Need for the Holy Spirit

The essential need for the Holy Spirit is quite clear. In Matthew 3:11 we read the words of John the Baptist:

I indeed baptize you with water unto repentance: but He that cometh after me is mightier than I, whose shoes I am not worthy to bear: He shall baptize you with the Holy Ghost, and with fire.

In Acts 2:38 we see a definite fulfillment of this passage. After Peter preached his great sermon on the day of Pentecost, the people asked what they should do. Peter said unto them, "...Repent, and be baptized every one of you in the name of Jesus Christ for the remission of sins, and ye shall receive the gift of the Holy Ghost."

The need for the Holy Spirit is demonstrated again and again by the apostles. In Acts 10:44 we read, "While

Peter yet spake these words, the Holy Ghost fell on all them which heard the word."

Please read the following carefully: Being filled with the Holy Ghost is not an experience that some Christians enjoy and others do not. Salvation is not a two-tiered experience. The concept of a second work of grace is more philosophical than biblical. A very prominent television minister, saying that if you have the Holy Ghost, you can then work for the Lord in a better way, and stand against the devil better, taught that some people are saved without the Holy Ghost and that others are saved with the Holy Ghost. Not so! The Holy Ghost is for all believers, not just some of us.

Baptism by the Holy Spirit is a distinct work, and it is a well-defined part of Christ's ministry. In Matthew 3:11 we read, "He shall baptize you with the Holy Ghost." In Acts 1:5 we read, "For John truly baptized with water; but ye shall be baptized with the Holy Ghost not many days hence."

In Acts 11:15-16, Peter recounts his encounter with Cornelius and his household, "...as I began to speak, the Holy Ghost fell on them, as on us at the beginning. Then remembered I the word of the Lord, how that He said, John indeed baptized with water; but ye shall be baptized with the Holy Ghost." As we look into the Word of God, it is clear that where people received the Holy Ghost, it wasn't some who received it; they all received it. In First Corinthians 12:13, it says, "For by one Spirit are we all baptized into one body...."

How do you get into the Body of Christ if you haven't been baptized into Him by the Holy Spirit? And if you are not baptized into the Body of Christ, how can you say you are saved? How do you become in Christ? Some say, "Just believe." But to truly believe means to be baptized into the Body of Christ.

I have used the phrase, "The baptism of the Spirit," several times, but this experience is described in several different ways. The Bible doesn't always say "baptism." In Acts 2:4 we read that they were all *filled* with the Holy Ghost. So instead of saying they were baptized with the Holy Ghost, it says they were filled with the Holy Ghost. In Acts 10:44 it says that while Peter yet spoke, the Holy Ghost fell on them. "And they of the circumcision which believed were astonished, as many as came with Peter, because that on the Gentiles also was poured out the gift of the Holy Ghost" (Acts 10:45). So here we see *filled*, *fell*, and *poured out*, but each one means to be baptized with the Holy Spirit. Each one refers to the same experience.

This union with Christ lasts forever. It is eternal. It lasts throughout life and continues even after death.

Chapter 19

Water Baptism

Baptism was instituted by the Lord Jesus Christ just prior to His ascension to Heaven. Our denomination believes in being baptized by immersion using the formula found in Acts where Peter was asked, "Men and brethren, what shall we do?" Peter said, "...Repent, and be baptized every one of you in the name of Jesus Christ for the remission of sins, and ye shall receive the gift of the Holy Ghost" (Acts 2:38). We firmly believe that baptism in the name of the Lord Jesus is in obedience to the command that Jesus gave in Matthew 28:19-20:

> *Go ye therefore, and teach all nations, baptizing them in the name of the Father, and of the Son, and of the Holy Ghost: teaching them to observe all things whatsoever I have commanded you....*

Most Christian denominations use the formula for baptism as it is found in Matthew. However, it is our view that the use of this formula–that is, the name of the Father, the Son, and the Holy Ghost—was never used by the apostles. Since it was never used by the apostles, it is not a part of apostolic teaching.

G.R. Beasley Murray, in his book *Baptism in the New Testament* says, "The use of the Trinitarian formula is late. Paul and the Acts of the Apostles uniformly represent baptism as administered in the name of the Lord Jesus Christ."[1]

Another writer, H.R. Vander, points out, "There is not one example in the whole New Testament literature of baptism taking place in the name of the Father, the Son and the Holy Spirit."[2]

James Hastings, the editor of "A Dictionary of the Bible," in Volume I, page 241, writes:

> "The institution of Christian baptism is to be dated from Christ's farewell command, 'Go ye and make disciples of all the nations, baptizing them into the name of the Father, and of the Son, and of the Holy Ghost' (Matthew 28:19). This command the Twelve do not attempt to carry out until they are free from the earlier charge (Luke 24:49). But directly they have 'been clothed with power from on high,' Peter begins to exhort the people to 'repent, and be baptized in the name of Jesus Christ unto the remission of their sins' (Acts 2:38), and with very great success. But here

1. G.R. Beasley Murray, *Baptism in the New Testament* (Grand Rapids, MI: William B. Eerdmans Publishing Company, 1962), 78.
2. Murray, *Baptism in the New Testament*, 82.

we are at once struck by the fact that, in spite of Christ's command to baptize into the name of the Trinity, no mention is made of the Trinity, but only of 'the name of Jesus Christ.' And this first and important record of Christian baptisms does not stand alone. The Samaritans who were converted by Philip were 'baptized into the name of Lord Jesus' (Acts 8:16). Peter at Caesarea commanded that Cornelius and those with him should be 'baptized in the name of Jesus Christ' (10:48). And the Ephesians disciples, when they were convinced of the insufficiency of John's baptism, were 'baptized into the name of the Lord Jesus' (19:5). Moreover, there is no mention in New Testament of any one being baptized into the name of the Trinity; and the expression 'baptized into Christ' (Romans 6:3, and Galatians 3:7; I Corinthians 1:13, 6:11) is more in harmony with the passages in the Acts than with the Divine command as recorded in Matt. 28:19 that "...The original form of words was 'into the name of Jesus Christ' or 'the name of Jesus Christ' or 'the Lord Jesus." Baptism into the name of the Trinity was a later development. After the one mention of it, Matthew 28:19, we do not find it again until Justin Martyr, and his formula is not identical with that in the Gospel...."[3]

3. James Hastings, "A Dictionary of the Bible," Vol. 1 (Hendrickson Publishers, 1988; originally published by T & T Clark, Edinburgh, 1898), 241.

In view of the fact that the apostles, who were obedient to the Lord Jesus Christ and were filled with the Spirit, never used the Trinitarian formula, and they administered baptism in the name of the Lord Jesus, we, too, follow the apostles' practice of baptizing in the name of the Lord Jesus Christ.

Chapter 20

Eternal Life

Jesus made it very clear in John 10:27-28 that we have eternal life. He said, "My sheep hear My voice, and I know them, and they follow Me: and I give unto them eternal life; and they shall never perish...." The word *sheep* is a metaphor for the children of God. The sheep belong to Christ because He gave His life for them. In John 10:11 Jesus said, "I am the good shepherd: the good shepherd giveth His life for the sheep." As I mentioned in another section, it has been said, "No one can take us out of the hand of Christ, but we can jump out of His hand of our own volition." Several questions are raised by that comment. What natural shepherd would allow his sheep to stray if he could prevent it? None. Equally true is the fact that God, who is able to keep us from falling, will not allow His sheep to fall into eternal damnation (see Jude 24). If, as the Bible says, God is able to keep us from falling, then why would Jesus, the good Shepherd, allow us to stray since He is able to prevent it?

Chapter 21

Free Will?

People talk about a free will, but when you stop to think about it, our will is not really and truly free. We have a will that enables us to decide what kind of car we want to buy, what kind of clothing we want to purchase, what we are going to wear today, and maybe whom to choose as our friends. But our will cannot be *totally* free, for if that were so, God's will would not be free. Why? Because God's will would then be subject to our free will.

The great French philosopher and atheist, Jean Paul Sartre, said, "If God exists I am not free, but I am free, therefore God does not exist." In other words, Sartre understood that if there is a God and that God is sovereign, our will must obviously then be subject to God's sovereign will.

Again, I say that Jesus tells us, "I am the good shepherd: the good shepherd giveth His life for the sheep" (Jn. 10:11). Why would He willingly allow His sheep to go astray? Remember, the words of Jesus are unconditional. He did not say, "If the sheep hear My voice...." He did not say, "If they follow Me...." He said, "They follow Me." (See John 10:27.)

Chapter 22

Election and Security

Let us turn to the apostle Paul's writings on the permanency of our union with Christ. This is sometimes referred to as the election and security of the child of God. As to his credentials, Paul wrote,

> *But I certify you, brethren, that the gospel which was preached of me is not after man. For I neither received it of man, neither was I taught it, but by the revelation of Jesus Christ* (Galatians 1:11-12).

Paul says the gospel that he preached was revealed to him by Jesus Christ, and this is what those of us who are troubled by some of the mysterious passages of the Bible must keep in mind.

In Ephesians 1:4-5, we read, "According as He hath chosen us in Him before the foundation of the world, that we should be holy and without blame before Him in love: having predestinated us unto the adoption of children by Jesus Christ to Himself, according to the good pleasure of His will." It is clear from this passage that we were chosen not at the time of conversion, but before the creation of the universe.

There are some who say that the choice indicated was not of individuals, but rather the Church as a whole. This, however, was not Paul's intent because he clearly addressed his letter to the saints of Ephesus. Had he meant this to refer to some large abstract group without any personal identity, he would have said so in the letter. We must never water down the clear meaning of the Bible in order to preserve some denominational position or preconceived idea.

Another point to note is that when God chose us to salvation, He did not choose us to live in sin and still go to Heaven. On the contrary, He chose that we should be holy and without blame before Him. Furthermore, this choice of those to be saved and our being predestined to the "adoption of children" was done, not according to any choice or merit on our part, but "according to the good pleasure of His will."

This means that God, in His sovereign will, has not only predestined us to the "adoption of children of Jesus Christ to Himself," but also "to be conformed to the image of His Son" (Rom. 8:29). And this He did, "...according to the purpose of Him who worketh all things after the counsel of His own will" (Eph. 1:11). Therefore, our salvation, or union with Christ, rests on the sovereign will of an all-powerful, kind, and giving God.

To press this point a little further, the apostle John tells us why he wrote one of his Epistles, "These things have I written unto you that believe on the name of the Son of God; that ye may know that ye have eternal life, and that ye may believe on the name of the Son of God" (1 Jn. 5:13). In Hebrews 5:8-9 we read, "Though He were a Son, yet learned He obedience by the things which He suffered; and being made perfect, He became the author of eternal salvation unto all them that obey Him."

God is not the author of a temporary salvation. If we have a salvation that we can lose, it is not permanent and can be only a temporary salvation. There is nothing in the Bible that speaks to a temporary salvation. And, I might add, the way that you can know that you are a chosen one of Christ, and not just a professor, is by following the words of Jesus, "If ye love Me, keep My commandments" (Jn. 14:15).

Chapter 23

By Their Fruit

None of us can truly say that we are saved eternally and continue to live in sin. Jesus said that you shall know them by their fruit (see Mt. 7:16-20). A good tree cannot bring forth corrupt fruit and a corrupt tree cannot bring forth good fruit (see Lk. 6:43). A tree is known by the fruit it bears. A good apple does not make a good apple tree. A good apple tree makes good apples.

We may confess that we are born again, and God who knows the heart will know that our confessions are true. However, the only way we can show our salvation to others is by the fruits we bear. This is what James meant when he said, "Even so faith, if it hath not works, is dead, being alone. ...shew me thy faith without thy works, and I will show thee my faith by my works" (Jas. 2:17-18).

Chapter 24

Security in Christ

God never intended for salvation to be a temporary thing. Paul's writings are so clear on this matter that I have difficulty understanding how they can be misunderstood. It seems to me that we would find great comfort in knowing that our salvation is secure in Christ. Instead, many ministers seem to find great joy in placing doubt in the minds of their parishioners, and their followers seem to enjoy being told that, although they may be saved at the moment, their salvation is only temporary–that there is a possibility of being lost in the end. I find very little comfort in this kind of doubt.

There is the false notion among many that the doctrine of the eternal security of the believers encourages people to live morally loose and careless lives. Nothing could be further from the truth. The Bible says, "Whosoever is born of God doth not commit sin; for His seed remaineth in him: and he cannot sin, because he is born of God" (1 Jn. 3:9). So if we are practicing sin that is a sure sign we are not saved.

For those who are truly saved, however, we can see God's love and care for us recorded in Romans 8. Someone once said that all the chapters of the Bible make up a glorious crown, but the eighth chapter of Romans is the brightest jewel of them all: Here we see God's unfailing purposes concerning His saints.

It tells us in unmistakable terms that the Holy Spirit helps us in our infirmities and makes intercession for us since we do not know what we should pray, and this intercession is made according to the will of God (see Rom. 8:26-27).

How the Lord loves His people! Romans tells us how God works in His sovereign grace to bring about His desired purposes. "And we know that all things work together for good to them that love God, to them who are called according to His purpose" (Rom. 8:28). I believe that passage, and I don't know how it would be possible for all things to work together for our good if any of His sheep ended up in the lake of fire. In Romans 8:29-30 we have what is known as the five golden links of salvation. Each one of these, as in a chain, are linked to the other. If one falls, they all fall. If one stands, they all stand. The five golden links of salvation are to be *foreknown*, *predestinated*, *called*, *justified*, and *glorified*. ("For whom He did foreknow, He also did predestinate to be conformed to the image of His Son, that He might be the firstborn among many brethren. Moreover whom He did predestinate, them He also called: and whom He called, them He also justified: and whom He justified, them He also glorified" [Rom. 8:29-30].)

We don't have our glorified bodies now, but this passage speaks as if we already had them because it is in the past tense. Our salvation is so certain that God speaks to it as if it had already been accomplished: "As it is written, I have made thee a father of many nations, before Him whom he believed, even God, who quickeneth the dead, and calleth those things which be not as though they were" (Rom. 4:17). Even though we are not yet glorified, God has called it as if it has already happened. It is totally clear that our union and bond with Jesus is forever settled.

So there will be no misunderstanding, I want to make a clear statement before I go any further: Being born again is an extraordinary act performed by God on the soul of man and woman. It is so stunning and remarkable that it is described as becoming a new creation in Christ. We have been delivered out of the power of darkness. We have been translated into the Kingdom of God's dear Son. We have been baptized into Christ. We have been buried with Him by baptism into death (see 2 Cor. 5:17; Col. 1:13; Rom. 6:3-4).

A person who has participated in this incredible experience could never, ever say, "Now that I am secure in Christ I can sin recklessly, with impunity, and never be lost." A child of God could never say that. To teach that one can live in sin and still go to Heaven is ridiculous.

A born-again child of God does not go through life trying to live in sin. And those who teach such drivel, demonstrate for all the world to see that they have never been born again.

Chapter 25

The Saint and Sin

Christ has taught us that our new birth manifests itself in obedience. Jesus said, "If ye love Me, keep My commandments" (Jn. 14:15). Further, John wrote in First John 3:9, "Whosoever is born of God doth not commit [practice] sin...." The King James version uses the word *commit* instead of *practice.* But newer translations use the phrase "does not habitually live in sin" or "docs not practice sin."

From the study of the King James version, we find that John did not mean that whosoever is born of God could not commit any act of sin because John said, "My little children, these things write I unto you, that ye sin not. And if any man sin, we have an advocate with the Father, Jesus Christ the righteous" (1 Jn. 2:1). Again John writes,

> *If we say that we have no sin, we deceive ourselves, and the truth is not in us. If we confess our sins, He is faithful and just to forgive us our sins, and to cleanse us*

> *from all unrighteousness. If we say that we have not sinned, we make Him a liar, and His word is not in us* (1 Jn. 1:8-10).

It is a sad thing to say that saints commit sin, but it is true. We know this to be a fact from the teachings of the Bible and from human experience. I have known many honest, sincere, but overzealous ministers who taught sinless perfection; they instructed their flock that they had to make 100 percent. In a sense, however, the child of God *is* absolutely perfect, but this perfection is the result of being cleansed by the shed blood of Christ, not by our own puny efforts.

The permanent nature of our salvation is pointed out by the apostle Peter:

> *Blessed be the God and Father of our Lord Jesus Christ, which according to His abundant mercy hath begotten us again unto a lively hope by the resurrection of Jesus Christ from the dead, to an inheritance, incorruptible, and undefiled, and that fadeth not away, reserved in heaven for you, who are kept by the power of God through faith unto salvation…* (1 Peter 1:3-5).

What more do we need as we read these tremendous passages of Scripture? Thomas Watson puts it this way, "Though the saints may come to that pass that they have but little faith, yet not to have no faith. Though grace may be abated, it is not abolished. Though the wise virgins slumbered, yet their lights did not quite go out."[1] And Dr. James Montgomery Boice

1. Thomas Watson, *A Body of Divinity* (Banner of Truth Publ., 1979), 521.

had this to say, "Perseverance does not mean that Christians are free from falling into sin because they are Christians."[2]

2. James Montgomery Boice, *Foundations of the Christian Faith* (Downers Grove, IL: InterVarsity Press, 1986), 520.

Chapter 26

The Unbreakable Connection

Now finally, concerning the security of the believer and the everlasting union between the believer and Christ, I want to point to some of the teachings of Jesus and Paul on this subject.

> *All that the Father giveth Me shall come to Me; and him that cometh to Me I will in no wise cast out. For I came down from heaven, not to do Mine own will, but the will of Him that sent Me. And this is the Father's will which hath sent Me, that of all which He hath given Me I should lose nothing, but should raise it up again at the last day. And this is the will of Him that sent Me, that every one which seeth the Son, and believeth on Him, may have everlasting life: and I will raise him up at the last day* (John 6:37-40).

Some people say, "Well, we know that Jesus would not cast out anyone, but it is possible for a person to leave Christ of his own accord." An argument like this is deceptive and misleading because if one could walk away from Christ or cast himself out of Christ, the Lord could not possibly say that it is the will of God that He should lose nothing. Nor could the Lord say that we will be raised up at the last day if it were possible for us, of our own free will, to dismiss ourselves out of the Body of Christ. Everything then would be dependent upon what *we* did. God could never make any specific statements of reality or certainty because we might decide to jump out of His hand. But this is not the case. The Lord said He would lose nothing and He would raise us up at the last day. These are the words of certainty.

To emphasize this, we should take a look at John 10.

> *My sheep hear My voice, and I know them, and they follow Me: and I give unto them eternal life; and they shall never perish, neither shall any man pluck them out of My hand. My Father, which gave them Me, is greater than all; and no man is able to pluck them out of My Father's hand* (John 10:27-29).

Let us pay close attention to verses 24-26:

> *Then came the Jews around about Him, and said unto Him, How long dost Thou make us to doubt? If Thou be the Christ, tell us plainly. Jesus answered them, I told you, and ye believed not: the works that I do in My Father's name, they bear witness of Me. But ye believe not, because ye are not of My sheep....*

Jesus told them that they were not His sheep because they did not believe. If they had believed, they would have been Christ's sheep and would have followed Him. These words are quite clear and quite plain.

All the apostles were great men, but I am of the opinion that the apostle Paul stands head and shoulders above them all. Paul testified that he was an apostle of Jesus Christ and received his commission from Him (see Gal. 1:1). He also stated that the gospel that he preached came to him by revelation of Jesus Christ (see Gal. 1:1-12). And concerning the final perseverance of the saints of God, Paul writes,

> *Who shall separate us from the love of Christ? shall tribulation, or distress, or persecution, or famine, or nakedness, or peril, or sword? As it is written, For thy sake we are killed all the day long; we are accounted as sheep for the slaughter. Nay, in all these things we are more than conquerors through Him that loved us. For I am persuaded, that neither death, nor life, nor angels, nor principalities, nor powers, nor things present, nor things to come, nor height, nor depth, nor any other creature, shall be able to separate us from the love of God, which is in Christ Jesus our Lord* (Romans 8:35-39).

Chapter 27

The Intermediate State

Our union with Christ remains intact even after death. The Scripture tells us there is a conscious existence after death for the saved and unsaved prior to the resurrection. In theological circles this is called "the intermediate state." In this state, saved persons are conscious of joy and peace. When a saved person dies, he or she goes directly into the presence of the Lord and has rest. This ceasing from labor is verified by Revelation 14:13: "...Blessed are the dead which die in the Lord from henceforth: Yea, saith the Spirit, that they may rest from their labours; and their works do follow them." A child of God does not need to have a dread or terror of death. If you have given your life to Christ, and you have faith in Him and believe in Him, it will certainly ease your passage as you leave this world into the next.

Those who are unsaved, however, have something to fear because at death they will go into a state of unrest and torment. Jesus gave a parable to this end (see Lk. 16:19-31). He spoke about a rich man and a man named Lazarus. The rich man was clothed in purple and dined sumptuously every day. Lazarus was a poor man in rags. He had no food and ate the bread that fell from the rich man's table. Lazarus was so poverty stricken and so weak from lack of food that he wasn't even able to keep the dogs away from him. Jesus said, "Moreover the dogs came and licked his sores" (Lk. 16:21b). One day Lazarus died and was carried by the angels into Abraham's bosom, which signifies a place of rest. The rich man died, "And in hell he lift up his eyes, being in torments..." (Lk. 16:23).

This story has nothing to do with poverty or riches. Souls do not go to Heaven simply because they are poor, and souls do not go to hell just because they are rich. It is clear from this story, or parable, as some call it, that upon death the saved go immediately into the presence of the Lord. Saints, at death, do not immediately receive their glorified or spiritual bodies because they have to wait for the first resurrection (see Rev. 20:5); but when the soul is separated from the body, it immediately enters into the presence of the Lord.

> *For we know that if our earthly house of this tabernacle were dissolved, we have a building of God, an house not made with hands, eternal in the heavens. For in this we groan, earnestly desiring to be clothed upon with our house which is from heaven. ... Therefore we are always confident, knowing that, whilst we are at home in the body, we are absent from the Lord: (For we*

> *walk by faith, not by sight:) We are confident, I say, and willing rather to be absent from the body, and to be present with the Lord* (2 Corinthians 5:1-2,6-8).

So when the souls of the saints of God take leave from their bodies, they are then present with the Lord.

I think the words of Jesus to the repentant thief on the cross are very instructive on this point. If you will look at Luke 23:42-43, when the thief said, "...Lord, remember me when Thou comest into Thy kingdom. And Jesus said unto him, Verily I say unto thee, Today shalt thou be with Me in paradise." This being present with Christ in the intermediate state is one of incompleteness. It will be made complete at the resurrection.

Chapter 28

The Final State

We will not be fully complete until our souls and spirits are joined to our resurrected bodies. We will reach our final state when the bodies of the saints are resurrected from the grave. In First Thessalonians 4:15-17 we read these words:

> *For this we say unto you by the word of the Lord, that we which are alive and remain unto the coming of the Lord shall not prevent them which are asleep. For the Lord Himself shall descend from heaven with a shout, with the voice of the archangel, and with the trump of God: and the dead in Christ shall rise first: then we which are alive and remain shall be caught up together with them in the clouds, to meet the Lord in the air: and so shall we ever be with the Lord.*

The saints who are alive will be changed. We can not enter Heaven with the body of flesh and blood; it is not equipped for Heaven. We can not rise through the air without an oxygen mask. This body will be changed. It will become a glorified body, like unto Jesus' glorified body. We will be caught up together with those who are dead and who had been resurrected, and then we shall forever be with the Lord.

This marvelous truth is reaffirmed in First Corinthians 15:51-57,

> *Behold, I shew you a mystery; We shall not all sleep, but we shall all be changed, in a moment, in the twinkling of an eye, at the last trump: for the trumpet shall sound, and the dead shall be raised incorruptible, and we shall be changed. For this corruptible must put on incorruption, and this mortal must put on immortality. So when this corruptible shall have put on incorruption, and this mortal shall have put on immortality, then shall be brought to pass the saying that is written, Death is swallowed up in victory. O death, where is thy sting? O grave, where is thy victory? The sting of death is sin; and the strength of sin is the law. But thanks be to God, which giveth us the victory through our Lord Jesus Christ.*

This union with Christ, this bond with Christ is unbreakable, indissoluble, forever and eternal. Those who have been born again have been chosen and called by the Almighty God.

Chapter 29

The Rule of Good Works

Someone may ask, "What role does good works play?" First, let us take a look at what good works *will not* do. Good works cannot bring salvation, for it is written, "Not by works of righteousness which we have done, but according to His mercy He saved us, by the washing of regeneration, and renewing of the Holy Ghost" (Tit. 3:5).

In the expression of our justification before God absolutely nothing is said about works. What is written is that, "Therefore being justified by faith, we have peace with God through our Lord Jesus Christ" (Rom. 5:1). Paul continues, "But that no man is justified by the law in the sight of God, it is evident: for, The just shall live by faith" (Gal. 3:11). We are saved by grace, through faith, and not by meritorious works (see Eph. 2:8-9). There is a place for good works, but not as a means of salvation.

Now let us look at what good works *will* do. Paul wrote that we should always be careful to maintain good works. He also said that we were created in Christ Jesus unto good works, and that God has ordained that we should walk in them (see Eph. 2:10).

The good works of the children of God signify to the world what God has already done in our hearts by faith in Jesus Christ. Always remember that apart from works, we cannot see the salvation that is in the believer's heart. The only way we can know that God has come into our lives is by the change of our hearts, which is made evident in the things we do. This is the real reason for the apostle James' sharp and incisive comment:

> *What doth it profit, my brethren, though a man say he hath faith, and have not works? can faith save him? If a brother or sister be naked, and destitute of daily food, and one of you say unto them, Depart in peace, be ye warmed and filled; notwithstanding ye give them not those things which are needful to the body; what doth it profit?* (James 2:14-16)

Suppose you visit a house where they have no food, no oil, nothing to heat the house, and you pray for them and then say, "Be warm, be full, claim it, claim it." Claim your food, claim your heat. James says, in effect, "Now that you have done all of this praying, if you leave and don't give them anything to fill their stomachs or to heat the house, what does it profit? They are just as cold and as hungry as when you came." James writes, "Even so faith, if it hath not works, is dead, being alone. Yea, a man may say, Thou hast faith, and I have works: shew me thy faith without thy works, and I will shew thee my faith by my works" (Jas. 2:17-18).

The purpose of works is to show others that you are a Christian. So when you find a person who claims to be a Christian but has no good works, then that person is an imposter. A person who claims to be saved and has no good works following him or her causes others to question whether his or her salvation is genuine.

The believer is called upon to display good works and to live a life of godliness; "...the grace of God that bringeth salvation hath appeared to all men, teaching us that, denying ungodliness and worldly lusts, we should live soberly, righteously, and godly, in this present world" (Tit. 2:11-12). We are called upon to deny the ungodliness of this world. To the Romans, Paul wrote,

> *I beseech you therefore, brethren, by the mercies of God, that ye present your bodies a living sacrifice, holy, acceptable unto God, which is your reasonable service. And be not conformed to this world: but be ye transformed by the renewing of your mind, that ye may prove what is that good, and acceptable, and perfect, will of God* (Romans 12:1-2).

Paul did not write this in order that people be saved. He wrote this to people who were already saved. We don't tell sinners to present their bodies as living sacrifices. That's like asking water to go up hill. We don't ask sinners to do what sinners can't do. People who present their bodies as living sacrifices are people who have been changed, people who have been born again, people who have a different relationship with God. Even though one may be eternally secure, each person still has a responsibility to obey the Lord in all respects and to show to the unbelieving world the power of Christ in his or her life.

Chapter 30

The Second Coming

Now that we have established the permanency of the union between Christ and His Church, let us address the second coming of the Lord. This is referred to as the Rapture of the Church. Every child of God should be looking for this event. I am convinced in my heart that Jesus is coming again. He's coming for His Church. There are people, some who claim to be Christians, who do not believe in the second coming. This should not come as a surprise. The apostle Peter gave solemn warning of this rejection of Bible truth when he wrote, "Knowing this first, that there shall come in the last days scoffers, walking after their own lusts, and saying, Where is the promise of His coming? for since the fathers fell asleep, all things continue as they were from the beginning of the creation" (2 Pet. 3:3-4). Peter goes on to say that those who deny the fact that the Lord will return are willingly ignorant (see 2 Pet. 3:5).

The coming of the Lord will be the greatest event that the world has ever known, for it will signal the triumphant return of Christ. He will gather His Church, which will include all those who died in Christ and all those who are alive when He comes. All those who died in Christ will be resurrected, and all the saints who are alive at His coming will be instantaneously changed. All will be caught up together to meet the Lord in the air (see 2 Thess. 4:14-17; 1 Cor. 15:52).

Do not be misled by false teachers who not only deny His virgin birth, but His deity as well. This leads to a further denial of the substitutional death of our Lord. We are encouraged, however, to hold onto these foundational truths, and we are told in Jude of the terrible judgment that awaits these false prophets.

> *Beloved, when I gave all diligence to write unto you of the common salvation, it was needful for me to write unto you, and exhort you that ye should earnestly contend for the faith which was once delivered unto the saints. For there are certain men crept in unawares, who were before of old ordained to this condemnation, ungodly men, turning the grace of our God into lasciviousness, and denying the only Lord God, and our Lord Jesus Christ. ... Woe unto them! for they have gone in the way of Cain, and ran greedily after the error of Balaam for reward, and perished in the gainsaying of Core. These are spots in your feasts of charity, when they feast with you, feeding themselves without fear: clouds they are without water, carried about of winds; trees whose fruit withereth, without fruit, twice dead, plucked up by the roots; raging waves of the sea, foaming out their own shame; wandering stars, to*

whom is reserved the blackness of darkness for ever. And Enoch also, the seventh from Adam, prophesied of these, saying, Behold, the Lord cometh with ten thousands of his saints, to execute judgment upon all, and to convince all that are ungodly among them of all their ungodly deeds which they have ungodly committed, and of all their hard speeches which ungodly sinners have spoken against Him (Jude 3-4, 11-15).

It certainly behooves us to be aware of these kinds of people and to remember the words of Jesus, "...If the blind lead the blind, both shall fall into the ditch" (Mt. 15:14).

At the closing days of His life on earth, Jesus met with His disciples and washed their feet. He taught them humility, He spoke of His betrayal by Judas, and then He comforted them with these words,

Let not your heart be troubled: ye believe in God, believe also in Me. In My Father's house are many mansions: if it were not so, I would have told you. I to to prepare a place for you. And if I go and prepare a place for you, I will come again, and receive you unto Myself... (John 14:1-3).

These are the words that fell from the lips of Jesus Christ Himself, "I will come again."

In the Book of Acts there is another prophetic utterance concerning our Lord's return:

And while they looked stedfastly toward heaven as He went up, behold, two men stood by them in white apparel; which also said, Ye men of Galilee, why stand ye

gazing up into heaven? this same Jesus, which is taken up from you into heaven, shall so come in like manner as ye have seen Him go into heaven (Acts 1:10-11).

And, of course the apostle Paul's letter to the Thessalonians gives us a clearer picture. He wrote,

> *For if we believe that Jesus died and rose again, even so them also which sleep in Jesus will God bring with Him. For this we say unto you by the word of the Lord, that we which are alive and remain unto the coming of the Lord shall not prevent them which are asleep. For the Lord Himself shall descend from heaven with a shout, with the voice of the archangel, and with the trump of God: and the dead in Christ shall rise first: then we which are alive and remain shall be caught up together with them in the clouds, to meet the Lord in the air: and so shall we ever be with the Lord. Wherefore comfort one another with these words* (1 Thessalonians 4:14-18).

Paul received the gospel message announcing the return of the Lord Jesus as a part of a revelation. To the Galatians he wrote, "But I certify you, brethren, that the gospel which was preached of me is not after man. For I neither received it of man, neither was I taught it, but by the revelation of Jesus Christ" (Gal. 1:11-12).

Chapter 31

The Great Resurrection

There is a connection between what Paul wrote in First Thessalonians and Jesus' words to Martha in John 11:23-25 concerning the death of Lazarus. Jesus said to Martha,

> *...Thy brother shall rise again. Martha saith unto Him, I know that he shall rise again in the resurrection at the last day. Jesus said unto her, I am the resurrection, and the life: he that believeth in Me, though he were dead, yet shall he live.*

The connection here is with First Thessalonians 4:16, "...the dead in Christ shall rise first." In John 11:26 Jesus said, "...Whosoever liveth and believeth in Me shall never die...." In First Thessalonians 4:17 it says, "Then we which are alive and remain shall be caught up together with them in the clouds, to meet the Lord in the air...." There is a group of people who will never die. They are those who will be present when the Lord Jesus Christ comes back again.

Finally, Paul writes of this great resurrection in First Corinthians 15:50-52. This is called the great resurrection chapter:

> *Now this I say, brethren, that flesh and blood cannot inherit the kingdom of God; neither doth corruption inherit incorruption. Behold, I shew you a mystery; We shall not all sleep* [Sleep is a synonym for dying], *but we shall all be changed, in a moment, in the twinkling of an eye, at the last trump: for the trumpet shall sound, and the dead shall be raised incorruptible, and we shall be changed.*

When Paul wrote, "For this corruptible must put on incorruption, and this mortal must put on immortality" (1 Cor. 15:53), he was thinking as all the early Christians did, and certainly as we ought, that he would be alive when the Lord came.

Chapter 32

The Crux of the Matter

As children of God, we are saved by grace. We are kept by God's power. All that is needed to live victoriously through life's day-to-day struggles has been provided. Because of this power, we can endure all that comes against us. And, in reflection, we will find our afflictions are light.

As Christians, we look forward to our final reward, the "weight of glory" (see 2 Cor. 4:17). As we enter into eternity we are secure in the promises of God that the blood of Jesus will cleanse us from all unrighteousness.

> *Furthermore then we beseech you, brethren, and exhort you by the Lord Jesus, that as ye have received of us how ye ought to walk and to please God, so ye would abound more and more* (1 Thessalonians 4:1).

IMAGE IS EVERYTHING

by Marvin L. Winans.

Yes, image IS everything! Does the image God has of you match the image you have of yourself? Society today suffers many social ills because of its lack of vision. Without an image we aimlessly grope about in life when we need to focus on what is true and accurate. We need the image that points us in the right direction—because *Image Is Everything*!

TPB-204p. ISBN 1-56043-262-4 (6" X 9") Retail $10.99

MAXIMIZING YOUR POTENTIAL

by Dr. Myles Munroe.

Are you bored with your latest success? Maybe you're frustrated at the prospect of retirement. This book will refire your passion for living! Learn to maximize the God-given potential lying dormant inside you through the practical, integrated, and penetrating concepts shared in this book. Go for the max—die empty!

TPB-196p. ISBN 1-56043-105-9 Retail $8.99

WHAT IS THE CHURCH COMING TO?

by LaFayette Scales.

Do you know what the Church is, and what its destiny and purpose are? In *What Is the Church Coming To?* you'll find fresh biblical insight, new studies, and exciting reflections on seven "pictures" of the Church that are found in the Bible. Rediscover today's Church as a powerful, living entity!

TPB-196p. ISBN 1-56043-169-5 Retail $8.99

ONE BLOOD

by Earl Paulk.

Step into the shoes of a man who dared to "rock the boat" by taking part in the civil rights movement deep in the heart of the South. Read in this book the astounding story of Earl Paulk's commitment to a Church in which every member is of "one blood" and one Spirit. See from a unique, inside perspective some of the greatest civil rights leaders of the century. A must-read book!

HB-176p. ISBN 1-56043-175-X (6" X 9") Retail $12.99

Internet:
http://www.reapernet.com